The Ella Zoo

Elizabeth Dimmette Coyne

illustrated by Valentina Felce

ISBN 978-0692328996

The text of this book is set in Minion Pro with titles in Henny Penny.

Printed and bound by
CreateSpace, Charleston, SC

for Ella

Introduction

When first I saw my little girl, I was amazed at her steadfast gaze at me
I gazed back and have gazed amazed continuously.
I've seen her grow and change into the most amazing creature.
I've seen her grow and change, with change the most common feature.
I've asked her almost every day, "Ella, what sort of creature are you?"
And I've stood amazed at my ever growing Ella Zoo.

The Caterpella

Swaddled so soon, ah

From this defenseless cocoon

May come a monarch

A Koella Bear

The moment someone asks
"Is that your daughter?"
When they see a sweet girl by my side,
With a dash and a streak
My little one is gone.
She climbs
And then
On my hip
Huddled up tight
Peering out
From one
Wide eye
Is a Koella Bear,
Quiet and shy.

The Girellaraffe

Oh they gain a surprising reach!
    Although it is a creature
    I've seldom seen
    I can tell a Girellaraffe lives here
    By the side boards and shelves
    Coffee tables and countertops
    Picked clean.

A growth chart that is naturally occurring,
    All too soon the only place
    I can find to store
    Anything is above
    The out-of-reach-line
    Where our verdant debris rises
    Now only inches below the ceiling.

An Ellaroo

Whenever it seems there is nothing to do
Waiting in line or waiting a turn
That is when she springs into being
And I realize what I have is an Ellaroo.

She hops on one foot, taps out her mirth
Or simply jitters a quick jack-hammer step.
She launches herself in exclamation mark shape
Repeatedly, joyously punctuating the earth.

She's a blur, a vertical whir of delight
Caught in her involuntary burst of pounce.
To say there's a spring in her step
Is an understatement alright…
Ellaroos bounce!

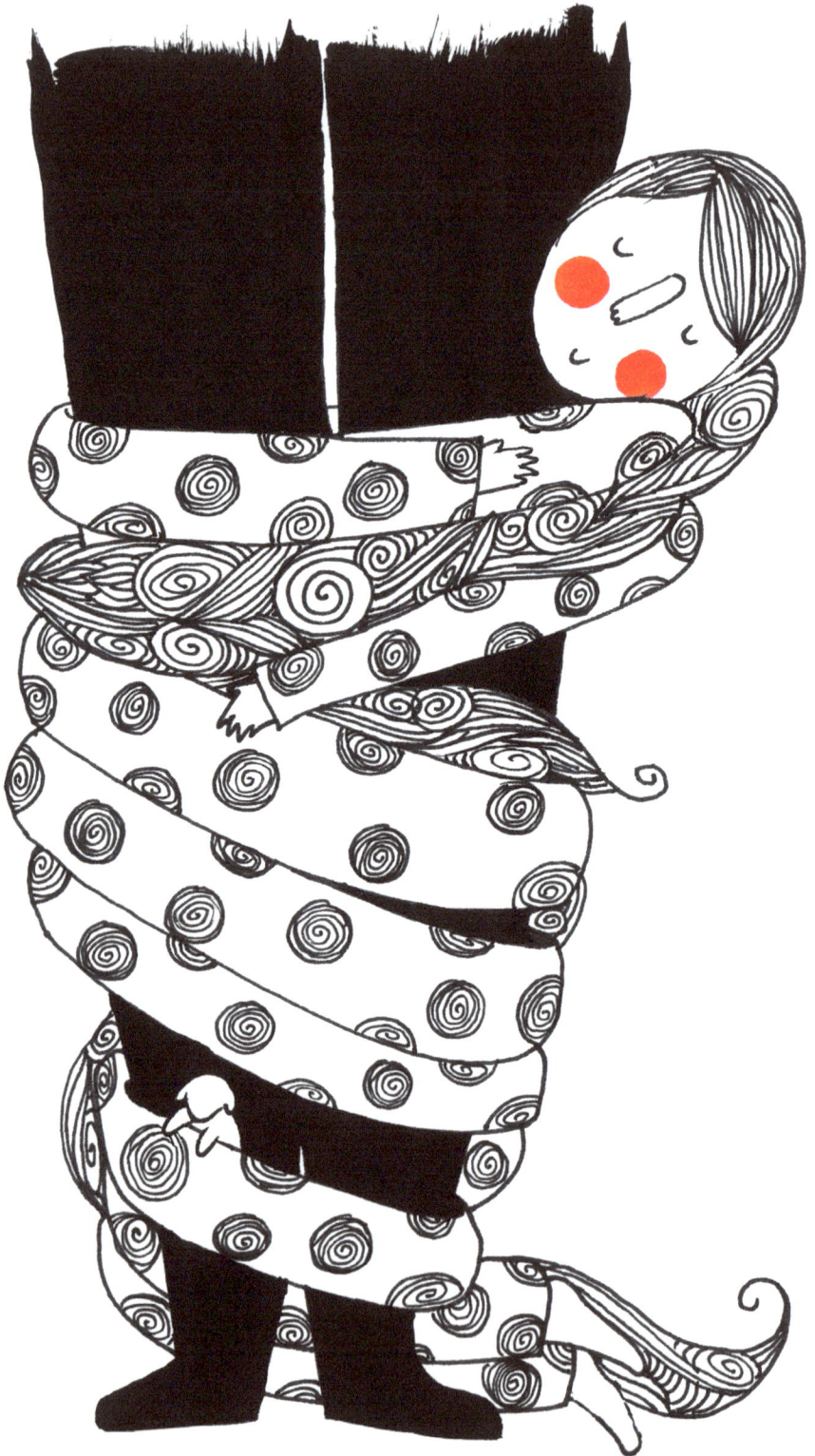

An Ellaconstrictor

We have dinner reservations, tickets and a sitter

I've scrubbed off craft glue, marker and glitter

Found an unstained blouse and a pair of flattering pants

Moving at top speed til, eee, 6:15, time to leave

Trip through the toy jungle and make for the door

Check the cells for their bars

Hand out emergency telephone numbers including ours

And turn to give the kids one last little kiss

When suddenly I'm under seize

Squeezed by a coil so tight I can't move

Let alone breathe…

    An Ellaconstrictor has unfurled from the floor.

The Pellagrine

With a falcon's keen vision
She spies a flaw
    "What is that, Mom?"
Her innocent sneer
A child's frank
    curiosity, that's all.
"A mole. You get them
when you grow older."
    "Oh."
And her eyes devour
    my vanity
    whole.

The Ellagator

Ellagators float on stiff and straight backs
With only their eyes above water
They lay perfectly still, their arms are slack
And they don't use the soap as they oughta
Rather than leave her to prune I've got to
Slowly enter the room and intervene
Carefully I know from times I've fought her
Nothing betrays her awareness of me
'Til I toss in a cloth that sinks unseen
And eyes trail me as I reach for the soap
Cautiously, 'cause her reflexes are keen
Then push it to her—with a thrash, I'm soaked.
    Forget coaxing from the sidelines, there's no doing.
    Now I'm all in, from tail to a good shampooing.

An Armadella

Full many a glorious morning have I seen,
As I sound the weekday wake-up call,
Her scurry to burrow back to her dreams
Under the duvet and into a ball.
There is no head on the pillow, no feet,
Just a mound shirking from the overhead light
Indignantly pleading to "Let me sleep!"
While pulling the sheets around herself tight.
With soft words, bright lights, then motherly threats
I vainly pry at her defensive curl
This armor is a Darwinian success
And an Armadella — nocturnal.
     And yet, a mother's made of tougher stuff,
     Whatever it takes, she'll be on that bus.

The Gazella

On the grass in the bright sun
　　See my Gazella run
Leaps off the bus when day's done
　　See my Gazella run.
With antelope legs — long, lean —
　　She takes chase gleefully
Or challenges all to a race
　　And sprints to the next tree.

On the fields in uniform
　　See my Gazella run
Stripes adorn the herd's sleek form
　　See my Gazella run
A soccer ball is involved
　　But the game's chase that's all
A pride of parents stands aside
Pick out their one with trained eyes
　　See my Gazella run.

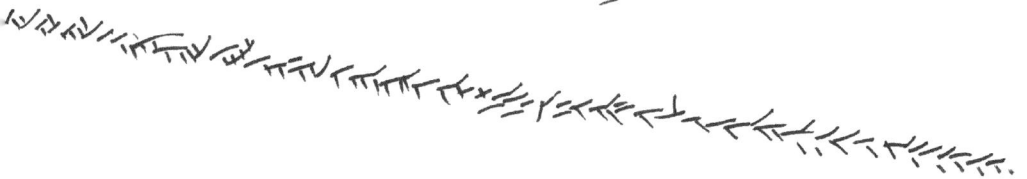

An Ellaphant

There are times when her silence grows alarmingly loud and

Her size swells with the disappointment or frustration she feels

Her brow wrinkles, her rosy cheeks wither to grey

Her mouth pinches tight below her nose

Her head droops with the weight of an elongating face

Until it is a trunk that reaches her toes

As she turns, she throws massive flat-footed slaps

Up the stairs, the house cowardly shakes

As an Ellaphant

Stomps

To her

Room

The Chamellaeon

She came home today
Clouded by a new hue
Her familiar form
Camouflaged in a
Classmate's sassy attitude
Brushed on by ancient
Survival instinct
And artistic slight of hand—
When unsure if foe or friend
The safest bet is…blend in.

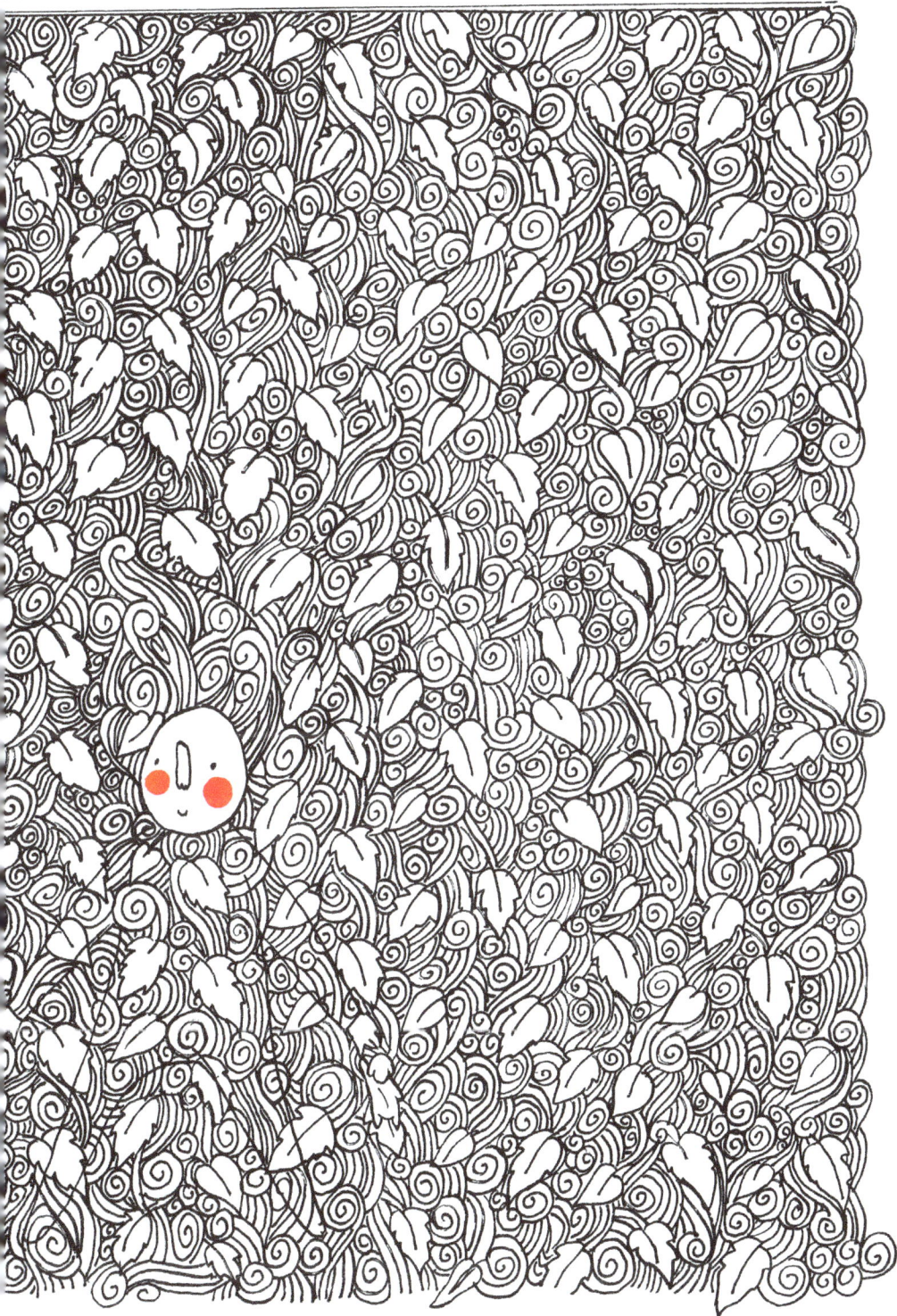

The Nightingella

We've had dinner

It's not yet late

Time for coffee

The guests

Brought cake

We grow

Contentedly

Slack

On the sofa

Is it the

Sound

Of an audience

Hushed

Or a darkened

House

That cues

The elegance

The wings

The quiet overture

When then

Our Nightingella

Sings

HIGH
GRUNT
= YES
ELLAS
ROOM
LOW

RULES:
NO BOYS
KNOCK
please!

STOP

DOGS
ARE
ALLOWED

GRRR
. . . .

AWAY

BEWARE

The Chinchella

How I long to stroke her soft fur
In my lap allow her to curl
Instead of the lonely burrow

Of her room where she roams at night
Where to her music she delights
Primping and preening out of sight

Tho' inquisitive as ever
And with her friends always clever
It is family she has severed

From her daily habitation
With territorial limitations
Here she's facing near extinction

Tho' occasionally she'll let me
In to stroke her head as nightly
I once did to a lullaby

The tune still ringing in my breast
Silently I lull her to rest
So I can this rare creature pet

And adore her. How lovely
And soft is my Chinchella.

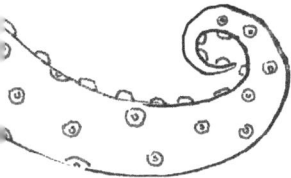

The Snaella

Ella dear, it is time to go!
We've a long list of things to do
And you have a lesson today
Let's stop by the store on the way
We need to hurry out the door.

Ella dear, you are quick as rust
Bring your brush with if you must
Do you realize how slow you are?
Ella dear, it is time.

Everyday her pace seems so slow
Pushing years then one day, I know
I don't want her to leave so fast
And when I try to hold her back
The keys, Mom — you need to let go.
Ella, oh dear, it is time.

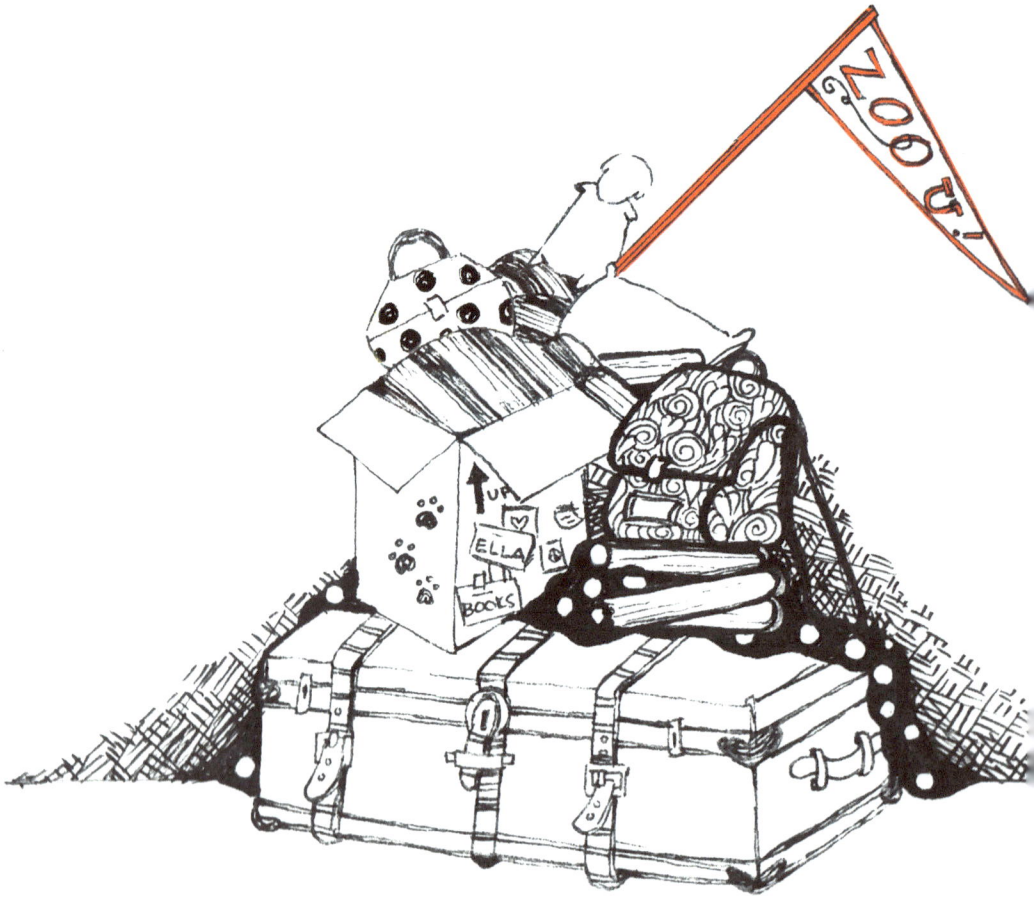

Ella

Rising through years
You seemed to pass
Through phases or that
You were playing out
A fantasy – exploring
Dreams. As such perhaps
I felt I had a part
In leading or shaping
The outcome. Or that
It was you who would
Make a decision
About what to be.
Looking back, now
I realize your
Inevitability.

You've been and you've grown
Magnificent,
Energetic and strong,
Watchful and quiet,
Curious and bold.
You are as shy and retiring
As you are feisty and headstrong.
You embrace those you love
Joyously. Just as you
Embrace your need for privacy.
You are an amazing creature.
You are she.
You are my Ella,
A woman
But still…
    Always my baby.

A Note from the Author

When writing *The Ella Zoo*, I enjoyed exploring different poetic forms. I began with a haiku for *Caterpella*. There are two sonnets. *Armadella* is a Shakespearean sonnet, the first line of which is Shakespeare's and *Ellagator* is a Spenserian sonnet. In *Gazella*, I echoed a poem by Robert Burns, *John Anderson, My Jo,* itself inspired by a popular song of his day. *Snaella* is a slightly modified rondeau. For the rest, I've employed couplets, triplets, a few odd rhyme schemes of my own invention and plenty of free verse, too. Together, the whole collection is something of a grand ode celebrating the wonder of all growing children, but especially my animal-adoring, sweet daughter, Ella.

— Elizabeth

Elizabeth Dimmette Coyne is the owner of S2dio comprised of S2dio Design, a graphic design business and S2dio Supplies, a mobile art supply store housed on a converted school bus. She lives in North Carolina with her husband, scenic designer and professor at UNC School of the Arts, John Coyne and their two childen, Ella and August.

A Note from the Illustrator

After dabbling in different fields, I discovered that my true passion lay in illustration and making toys from those illustrations. I love creating and celebrating characters that are unique, strange and wonderful.

BlueRaspberryDesigns.com is my online boutique where you can find my hand-crafted, one-of-a-kind, art dolls, including an Ella Zoo doll. I am currently a freelance designer, blogger and painter who finds joy in taking on all sorts of projects.

– Valentina

Valentina Felce is a design graduate of UNC School of the Arts. Valentina's illustrations were created on bristol using Pigma Micron pens.

www.ingramcontent.com/pod-product-compliance
Lightning Source LLC
LaVergne TN
LVHW010036070426
835513LV00005B/123